Thank you for reading our Chinese Heritage Songbook. We created the Heritage Songbook Series to promote musical understanding between children, parents, and educators around the world.

We hope you spend many happy hours with the children in your care singing these songs and listening to the accompanying recordings at montessorimusiclab.com. There, you'll also find coloring pages and other printable activities for all the books in our Heritage Songbook Series.

We've also included color-coded sheet music so young instrumentalists can play and sing along. We recommend using colored rainbow bells that match up with our notation system, but you can also use colored stickers on piano keys or ukulele frets if you would like.

Happy Music-Making!

From the Montessori Music Lab

www.montessorimusiclab.com

TABLE OF CONTENTS

CHINESE HERITAGE SONGBOOK

HUĀNYÍNG! (欢迎)
WELCOME TO CHINA!

More people live in China than in any other country on Earth with a population of 1.3 billion. That's more than four times as many people living in the United States!

KAZAKHSTAN

MONGOLIA

KYRGYZSTAN

NORTH KOREA

TAJ.

Beijing

PAK.

SOUTH KOREA

CHINA

NEPAL

INDIA

BANGL

BURMA

LAOS

China is one of the oldest civilizations on the planet. Its rich history of art, science, philosophy and music have influenced and inspired people around the globe for thousands of years. Chinese inventions include paper, gunpowder, the magnetic compass, and silk. China continues its history of invention today with cutting edge development of medicine and technology.

The official language of China is Mandarin, but depending where in the country you are, you may hear one of nine other major dialects that are like their own language. Mandarin uses four different tones to change the meaning of the same words. Watch your tone, or you could accidentally call your mother a horse!

China is also home to thousands of species of animals, plants, fish, and amphibians. Its most famous animal is the giant panda, which can only be found in China.

FÈNG YÁNG HUĀ GǓ (鳳陽花鼓)
FENG YANG FLOWER DRUM

左手锣右手鼓
ZUǑ SHǑU LUÓ YÒU SHǑU GǓ
I CAN PLAY A DRUM! I CAN PLAY A GONG!

手拿着锣鼓来唱歌
SHǑU NÁ ZHE LUÓ GǓ LÁI CHÀNG GĒ
PLAY THEM TOGETHER AND SING "FENG YANG!"

别的歌儿我也不会唱
BIÉ DE GĒ ÉR WǑYĚ BÙ HUÌ CHÀNG
NO OTHER SONG WOULD I EVER WANT TO SING

11

只会唱个凤阳歌
JǏ HUÌ CHÀNG GÈ FÈNG YÁNG GĒ
Only my Feng yang, play and play again!

凤拉凤阳歌来
FÈNG LA FÈNG YÁNG GĒ LÁI
Feng yang, Feng yang, play and play again!

12

得儿嘟当飘一飘
Drrr lāng dāng piāo yī piāo
得儿嘟当飘一飘
Drrr lāng dāng piāo yī piāo

13

得飘 得飘 得飘得飘飘一得
DRR PIĀO, DRR PIĀO, DRR PIĀO DRR PIĀO PIĀO YĪ DRR

飘飘飘一飘
PIĀO PIĀO PIĀO YĪ PIĀO!

FENG YANG FLOWER DRUM

CHINESE TRADITIONAL

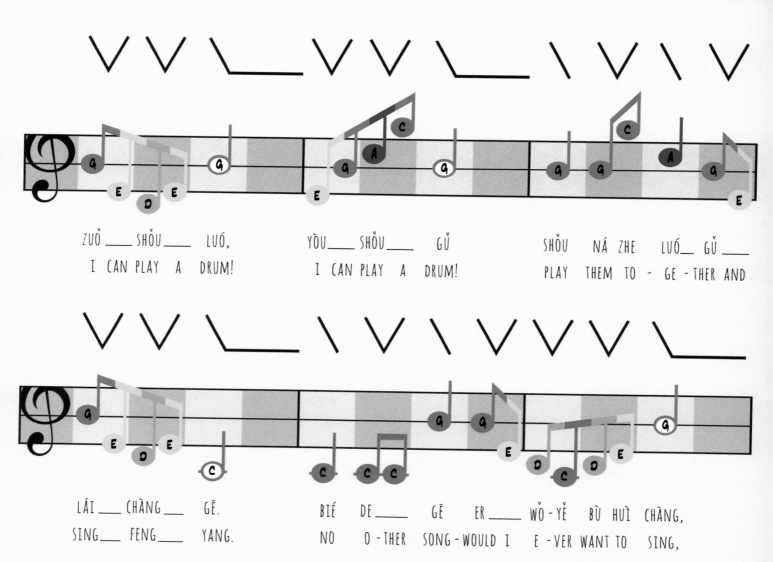

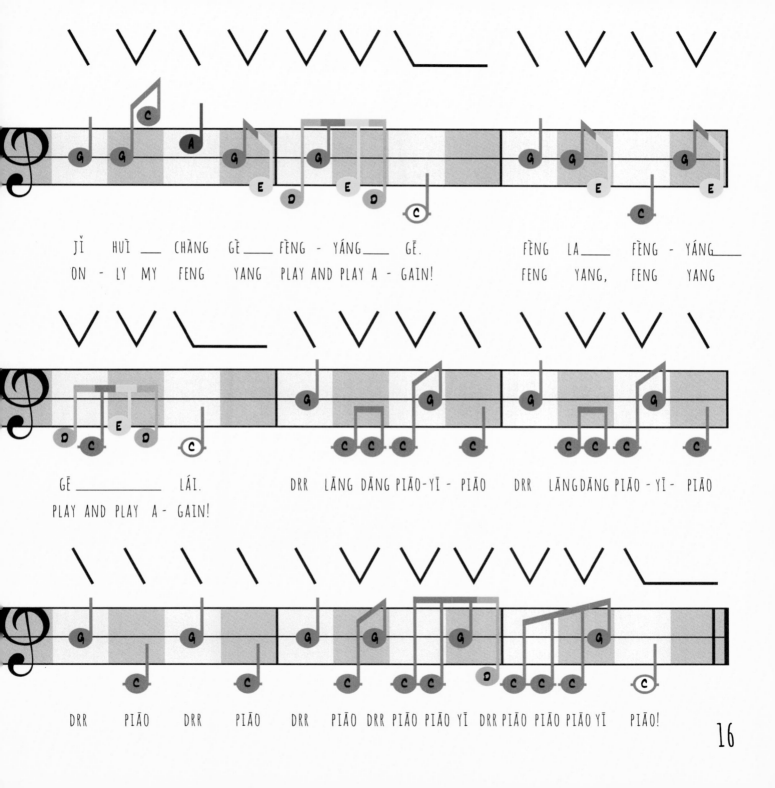

JǏ HUÌ ___ CHÀNG GĒ___ FÈNG - YÁNG___ GĒ.   FÈNG LA___ FÈNG - YÁNG___
ON – LY MY FENG   YANG   PLAY AND PLAY A - GAIN!   FENG   YANG,   FENG   YANG

GĒ _____ LÁI.   DRR LĀNG DĀNG PIĀO-YĪ - PIĀO   DRR LĀNGDĀNG PIĀO - YĪ- PIĀO
PLAY AND PLAY A - GAIN!

DRR   PIĀO   DRR   PIĀO   DRR   PIĀO DRR PIĀO PIĀO YĪ DRR PIĀO PIĀO PIĀO YĪ   PIĀO!

16

MÒLIHUĀ (茉莉花)
JASMINE FLOWER

好一朵美丽的茉莉花

HĂO YĪ DUŎ MĔI LÌ DE MÒLIHUĀ

Beautiful petals on the jasmine flower

18

芬芳美丽满枝桠

FĒN FĀNG MĚI LÌ MǍN ZHĪ YĀ
SEND YOUR PERFUME THROUGH THE AIR

19

又香又白人人夸

YÒU XIĀNG YÒU BÁI RÉN RÉN KUĀ

SWEET AND FRAGRANT, CLEAN AND FAIR

20

让我来将你摘下
RÀNG WǑ LÁI JIĀNG NǏ ZHĀI XIÀ
BRAID A BLOSSOM IN YOUR HAIR

送给别人家
SÒNG GĚI BIÉ RÉN JIĀ
PICK UP ANOTHER ONE TO SHARE

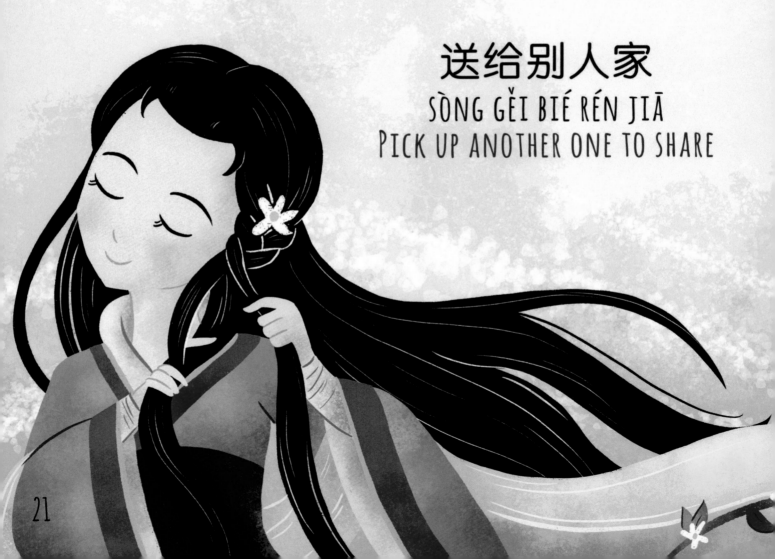

茉莉花呀茉莉花

MÒLIHUĀ YA MÒLIHUĀ

JASMINE FLOWER, MY JASMINE FLOWER

JASMINE FLOWER

CHINESE TRADITIONAL

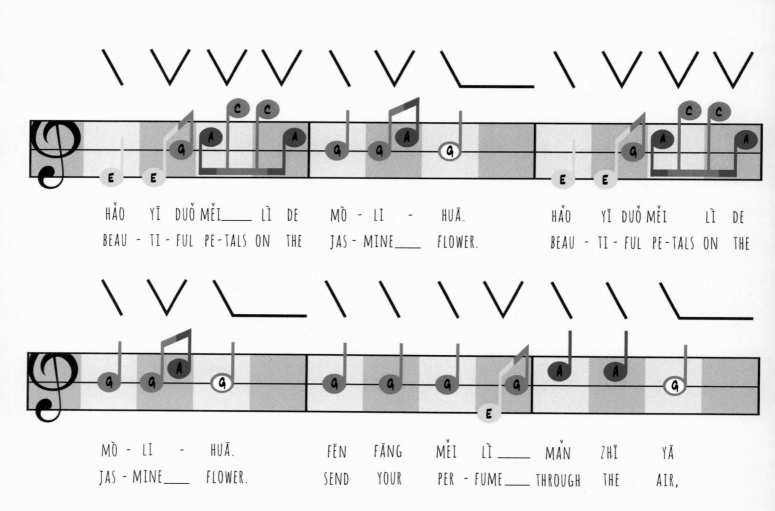

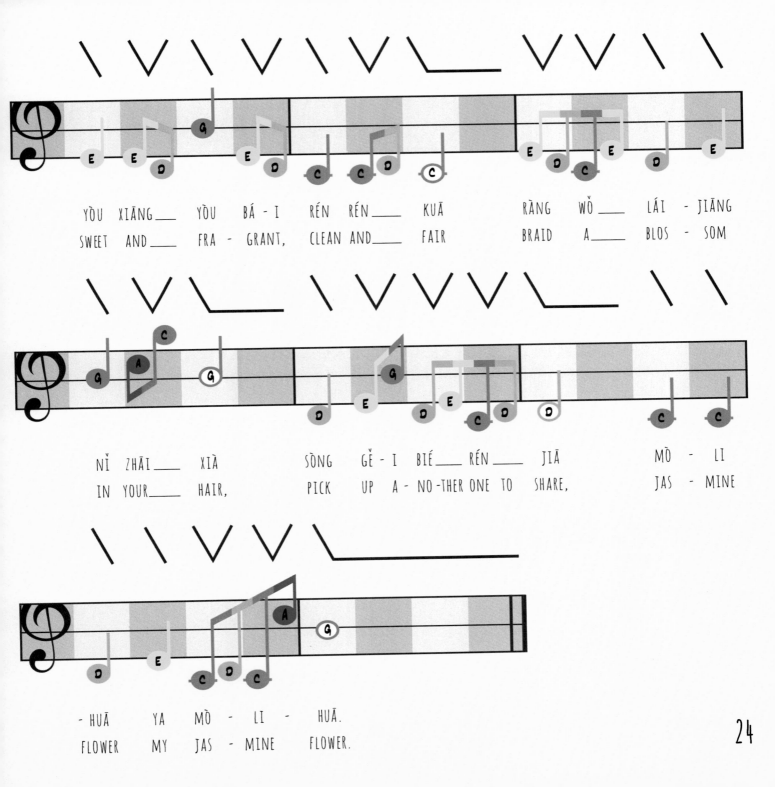

HǓOCHĒ KUÀI FĒI
(火车快飞)
FASTER, TRAIN!

火车快飞，火车快飞
Hǔochē kuài fēi, hǔochē kuài fēi
Faster train, go faster train

飞过高山，越过小溪
FĒI GUÒ GĀO SHĀN, YUÈGUÒ XIǍO XĪ
GO OVER BROOK AND OVER MOUNTAIN!

一天要跑几百里…
YĪ TIĀN YÀO PAO JǏ BǍI LǏ
FASTER, FASTER, FLY, FLY, FLY!

开到家里，开到家里
KĀI DÀO JIĀ LǏ, KĀI DÀO JIĀ LǏ
MANY, MANY, MILES, WE GO MANY, MANY, MILES

27

妈妈看了真欢喜

MĀMA KÀN LE ZHĒN HUĀNXǏ

WE GO HOME TO MAMA STANDING BY!

FASTER, TRAIN!

CHINESE TRADITIONAL

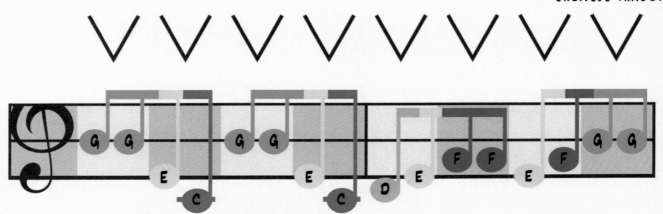

HUǑ - CHE KUÀI FEI   HUǑ - CHE KUÀI FEI   FEI - GUÒ GĀO SHĀN, YUÈ - GUÒ XIǍO XĪ
FAST - ER TRAIN, GO FAST - ER TRAIN GO   O - VER BROOK AND O - VER MOUN - TAIN!

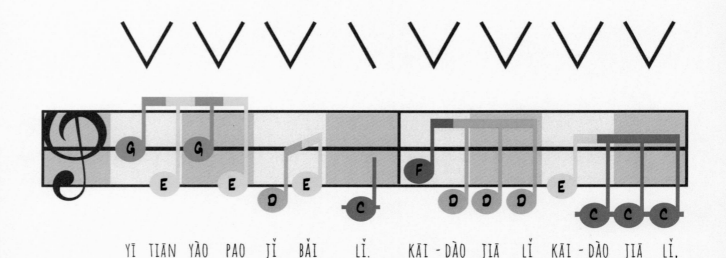

YĪ TIĀN YÀO PAO JǏ BǍI   LǏ.   KĀI - DÀO JIĀ LǏ KĀI - DÀO JIĀ LǏ,
FAST - ER, FAST - ER, FLY, FLY, FLY!   MA - NY, MA - NY, MI - LES, WE GO

31

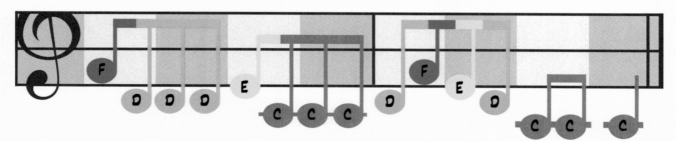

KĀI -DÀO JIĀ LǏ KĀI -DÀO JIĀ LIA, MĀ -MA KÀN LE ZHĒN HUĀN - XǏ

MA -NY, MA -NY, MI -LES WE GO HOME TO MA - MA STAND -ING BY!

YǓ BÙ SǍ HUĀ, HUĀ BU HÓNG
(雨不洒花花不红)
RAIN WILL HELP THE FLOWERS GROW

哥是天上一条龙
Gē shì tiānshàng yītiáo lóng
Brother is a dragon high . . .

妹是地下花一蓬
Mèi shì dìxià huā yī péng
Sister waits for him at home.

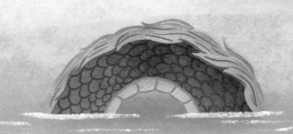

龙不抬头不下雨
LÓNG BÙ TÁITÓU BÙXIÀ YǓ
BROTHER TURNS AND BRINGS THE RAIN

雨不洒花花不红

YǓ BÙ SǍ HUĀ HUĀ BU HÓNG.

AND THE RAIN WILL HELP THE FLOWERS GROW.

龙不抬头不下雨
Lóng bù táitóu bùxià yǔ
Brother turns and brings the rain

雨不洒花花不红
YǓ BÙ SǍ HUĀ HUĀ BU HÓNG.
AND THE RAIN WILL HELP THE FLOWERS GROW.

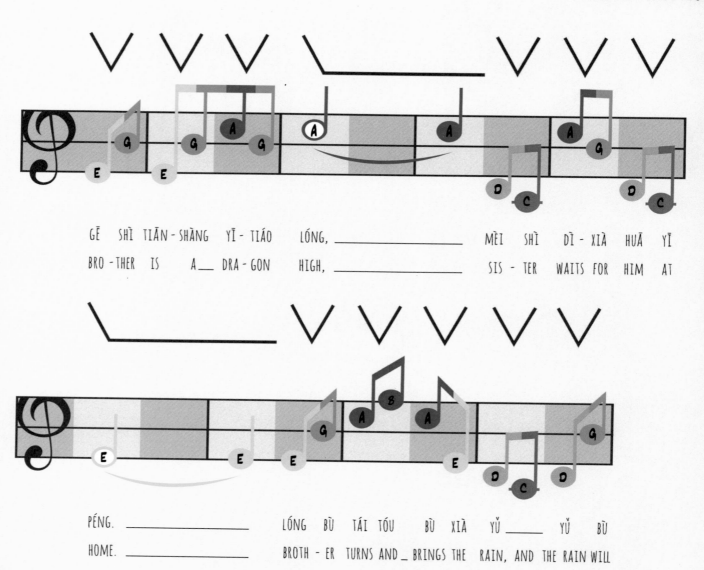

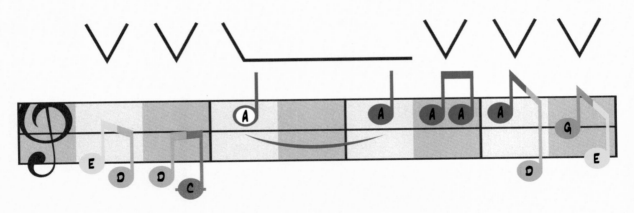

SǍ HUĀ HUĀ BU HÓNG. _____ LÓNG BÙ TÁI-TÓU BÙ-XIÀ

HELP THE FLO - WERS GROW. _____ BROTH - ER TURNS AND BRINGS THE

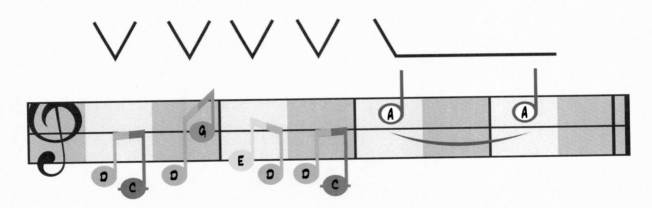

YǓ _____ YǓ BÙ SǍ HUĀ HUĀ BU HÓNG. _____

RAIN, AND THE RAIN WILL HELP THE FLOW - ERS GROW. _____

Made in the USA
Lexington, KY
29 December 2017

THE CHINESE HERITAGE SONGBOOK COLLECTS FOUR CLASSIC CHILDREN'S SONGS FROM THE HISTORY OF CHINA FOR YOUNG LEARNERS ALL OVER THE WORLD. EACH FULLY-ILLUSTRATED SONG INCLUDES LYRICS IN SIMPLIFIED CHINESE CHARACTERS, PINYIN, AND SINGABLE ENGLISH TRANSLATION. COLOR-CODED SHEET MUSIC FOR RAINBOW BELLS AND ACCOMPANYING RECORDINGS ON CD AND SPOTIFY MAKE IT EASY FOR THE WHOLE FAMILY TO PLAY AND SING ALONG TOGETHER.

MONTESSORI MUSIC LAB IS BASED IN CAMBRIDGE, MA AND PRODUCES EDUCATIONAL MUSIC CONTENT FOR YOUNG PEOPLE WORLDWIDE.

WWW.MONTESSORIMUSICLAB.COM

PRINTED IN THE UNITED STATES

ISBN 9781981667802

90000

9 781981 667802

What is a
PATKA?

Written by
Tajinder Kaur Kalia

Illustrated by
Yuribelle

Ypma.